Ignorance
is Expensive

Ignorance
is Expensive

Osei Owusu Stephen

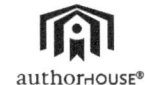

authorHOUSE®

AuthorHouse™
1663 Liberty Drive
Bloomington, IN 47403
www.authorhouse.com
Phone: 1-800-839-8640

Published by AuthorHouse   05/19/2012

ISBN: 978-1-4685-8243-7 (sc)
ISBN: 978-1-4685-8244-4 (e)

CONTENTS

ACKNOWLEDGEMENT

TO THE GLORY OF GOD

This book is dedicated to my lovely daughter Maggie-King Osei Owusu, and to my wife Mrs. Vida Osei Owusu for her immense contribution in many ways. Thank you!

The next acknowledgement is to Pastor Geoffrey King and family, and the entire members of Radcliffe Baptist Church for your love, prayers and support in many ways.

Another sincere acknowledgement to Donald Morrison my best friend and a former seminarian at London Theological seminary whose contribution made the publishing of this book possible.

To my spiritual father and mentor who without I could not have reach where I am-Rev. Enoch Kwabena Nketiah of Global Deliverance Baptist Church. A father through whom I came to know the Lord, taught me the art of soul wining, prayer and fasting and everything. Dear dad how can I ever pays you? Your immense contributions for my life both spiritual and physical are beyond words. Dear dad, I love you and my salute to this man of faith, prayer and fasting and respect. I believe your contribution to my life is an eternal memorial before God.

PREFACE

How will you explain to people that **ignorance is expensive** and a curse as well? In what ways can such a message be put across to posterity trying to let them understands that **Knowledge is power** which must be embraced as a cherished culture? It is a serious note the world but especially to Africa that ignorance blended in a culture of **indifference** is destructive!

The noble desire of sending warning signal against ignorance, illiteracy and corruption which have been the major cause of most Africans unnecessary poverty, deprivation and hardships could have been avoided had access to education for all been made possible and accessible to every African citizenry. Then I sincerely believe Africa could have had a better story yet it is never too late to for our emergence or rebirth in many ways. All that we need is a determinant culture for positive change.

To pinch your self is not easy especially when pride could be dented yet for the sake of posterity Africa can tell her own story through our sordid experiences which the continent had underwent over centuries without leaving behind the lessons from ignorance as a major contributory factor to the clouds of gloominess which had settled on Africa.

A cursory look at Africa of her endowed natural resources those tapped and untapped and the infinite wealth of human potentials left unharnessed due to lack of a better education of our people is a sore indictment. This continent as matter of fact should not have been on our knees as beggars always begging donor nations and financial institutions for bail-outs. Because if it isn't bad governance, endemic culture of corruption with impunity, failed institutions and illiteracy Africa should have been the bread basket of the world.

But an independent Africa is nothing more than just in name because in practice we've imperceptibly placed our necks in the chains of neo-colonialism which Africa fought against in the name of colonialism and slavery. We should candidly ask ourselves why all these scars of poverty, servitude, hardships, civil wars, misery and subservience? The world have its version depending on a particular perspective it looks at Africa but we as Africans as I said earlier are the very best people to narrate our stories of their enormous challenges and the inundating complex issues Africa faces every day. I therefore in humility challenge the illustrious sons and daughters of Africa not to cease in blowing the trumpets of warning that indeed, ignorance is very expensive and Africans are paying the price of ignorance displayed in many ways **painfully**.

Ignorance in part can be a universal disease because it has a relative dimensions as well. Therefore it is time the world has to be warn whether the West, Asia or Africa that we ought never to travel the path of ignorance nor cultivate the habit of indifference. But borne with godly fear and desire for humane living humanity pursue the path of practical knowledge. If Africa can cultivate the spirit of nationalism with sobriety and sincerity as our hallmark, forge ahead for the best then god will surely be on our side for the dawn of a new day because knowledge is power but divine knowledge in Christ is life eternal indeed

INTRODUCTION

A culture of silence is an environment where daring to complain or raise questions virtually amount to the breaking of the taboo's of the status quo. This has been the imperceptible cultural straightjacket—a norm of the masses. Such attitude over the years has been a detrimental to Africa's progress and economic growth. People who are critical or very outspoken to the status quo of the decadence of our times are usually perceived as non patriotic, liberal or inciting. This consequently has paved a path of despondency this entrenched atmosphere of silence yet quizzical.

Apprehension, direct or indirect repression in the course of time can metamorphose into social upheaval. Such tensions are usually reflective through the various political and the ethnic tensions going on in the world. Liberty of expression is a fundamental Human Right which maintains social and ethical values as intrinsic necessity. Hence one's non-contradictory right to query or be queried without fear or inhibition is a progressive sage for development.

To be honestly introspective evokes the spirit for a positive change and this is a culture most Africans have not inculcated in our developmental framework. It is in this regard which has rendered most of the Africa society immunity from probity and accountability, because no one is made to feel responsible. It ought to be understood that the kind of questions one asks determines his or her reflective attitude. Africans need to develop the culture of a comprehensive evaluation and assessment which inures for redresses. This is the path for progress, innovation, and creativity. We need to embark on self exploratory adventure, to follow the path of pondering our ways and attitudes ***whether we are the very cause of our woes***? Urgent awareness is what Africa needs!

Every culture where children are either hush or were reprimanded for being inquisitive is susceptible of suffering from inhibition tendencies. It is established fact that asking good questions have the ability to change one's focus, mindset or outlook. Thus to my candid opinion questions be merely subjective or for philosophical score but to provoke genuine sense for awareness which calls reparations or solutions. In that regard we ought to nurture an open mindedness orientation lifestyle.

Every nation or continent tries its best to identify disaffecting factors in order to come out for solutions and Africa should not an exception for we are and not wired for failure but for success. This is the goal of this little book and it is my solemn prayer that it will create a sense of awareness and acceptance of the fact that Africa's failures of underdevelopment is also partly contributed by ignorance's and attitudinal lapses in many ways.

CHAPTER ONE

THE LEGACY OF CORRUPTION IN AFRICA

Corruption is an international social disease but Africa is the epic center, and the sub-Saharan Africa is the haven where it is spawn, breeds and nurtured. At the heart of the endemic poverty, high illiteracy rate, lack of better social services like health, shoddy works, lack of good drinking, civil strives, ethnic tensions, rebels activities, and various coup d'états in most Africa states, shoddy works stems from corruption.

'In Cameroon, government contracts are being given out on the percentage basis. Once the contract has been awarded workers need to bribe contractors to in order to have a job. The government is aware of all this but it is this corrupt system that is keeping the them in place, they don't bother to do anything about it' Linus, Cameroonian

'If we want to reduce corruption we have to reduce the number of children born in a society' Chandru Narayan, USA

'How do you expect somebody with a family who is existing on his meager salary to survive? Corruption starts with us all'. Cornelius A. Gligui, Ghana

'Corruption is rapidly becoming part of us especially in Africa. In Zambia for instance you cannot get a job or a place ion school if you don't corrupt someone in higher authority. We all have a part to play in order to eradicate this vice' Wamuzi Lifuna, Lusaka Zambia

'The Kenya government effort in its fight against corruption is comparable to the effort of one who digs a hole while simultaneously filling it up. Its effort will never bear fruit unless it rids itself of those corrupt government officials that where recycled back into the new government from the previous one'. Mzee Kobe US Kenya

Here in the Gambia corruption is fuelled by a deep rooted norm we call 'MASLAhA' an expression that when mentions makes every average Gambian cool down and usually forgives or leaves what they are doing. Even the worst corrupt practices are sometimes condoned because of our maslaha attitude' Dawda Alpha Jallow, Gambia.

Corruption is a universal social disease which cut across every society or institution but with especially in Africa it has found a haven to breed and reproduce itself. Take for example the unrest in the Niger Delta and how the oil companies like Shell and others with the main culprit the Nigerian government has left the state in lurch. For almost five decades of oil extraction and the billions the Nigeria government had been making *'It should be a paradise, but the devastation in Nigeria's oil-rich Ogoniland remains numbingly sad'* New Africa report. A 80 years old man report 'As a result of the oil pollution, our youths are unable to fish or engage in farming, which are the main occupations in this area. So they have nothing to look forward to'.

Such a region ravaged by poverty and ecological destruction with people occupation destroyed most of the youths are vulnerable to this extremist and rebels radical ideologies, easy pick target and easy pick to join armed groups in the region because of frustration and poverty. Rebels or armed groups activities not justifiable in no terms but the question ought to be asked, what provoke these dissensions?

When most African governments take advantage of the states through corruption and nepotism isn't these actions are enough incentive to fuel anger, repression and abuse of the national cake while some few people at the helm of affairs take advantage to abuse and impoverish the masses in the name of governance of party politics in Africa? are the things to expect—unrest, wars and secessions?

Considering what is happening in Delta State oil region in Nigeria and the condition of the people and the unrest. We should ask,

'Has African ever considered the <u>consequences</u> of corruption in all its forms?

Why is ignorance so expensive? We must find it out from the face of Africa in its deplorable state of affairs; the lack of stable progressive development and economic under achievement. When you look at what is going on in Darfur and between the Sudanese government and the South Sudan government and the recent bombings. How can the world calls for peace where there is no justice?

Corruption is so typical of Africa. It has become a social virus and a moral gangrene like cancer eating away every fabric of moral ethics and social responsible consciousness in leadership and citizenry. The display of corruption in governance and institutional failures which should have helped curb the menace of corruption has itself been tainted with corruption. Especially with the political ideology that most of Africa governance practiced as 'the winner takes it all'.

How can the IGP who is the Inspector General of Police be fair in their operations to opposition when for the sake of incumbency powers are abuse? And the opposition see that there is no fairness because the security agents with the boss playing in tandem to the dictates of their power that be? The irony of Africa's ignorance through abuse of power and political corruption is so satirical. Sometimes you wonder why Africa loves to be applauded by our colonial masters in the name of figures for their very interest why the ordinary citizen in Africa knows in truth that things are not what they are. Sadly, it is just a political gimmick of higher ignorance that most Africa political leadership displays to the world.

But truth can never be chained or gage by the chains of repression.

Is oil a curse or a blessing to Africa?' An old man in Nigeria reported 'when oil in Nigeria was discovered we were made to clap our hands and dance like children, but before the discovery things were better than now' Is it a pessimistic stance to contemplate on Ghana's recent oil findings. Well, maybe the economic community with the China penetrating Africa with their financial aids and low quality services and products which never would never be accepted in the European or the American markets are most welcome in Africa even including toxic waste which killed a lot of people in Ivory Coast, Why? The answer is simply this because

The avarice of corruption is so virulent to heal.

In Africa we don't hail any new finding whether it is oil or gold. The recent oil extraction in Ghana has not contributed to anything to better to the ordinary Ghanaian. Maybe the politicians can quotes their single

GDP achievements from both the former and the current government but always

Truth is obvious. It is only those with delusion and illusion who calls the night as day

Africa has whatever it got to be successful and helps its people with decent and adequate lively hood. Consider the diamonds, coppers, bauxite, manganese, oil, uranium, gold, aluminum and other minerals that God has blessed Africa with none of these has really contributed much to the ordinary African citizenries in terms of social benefits the our governments has to provide the people.

A visit to various mining communities in Africa will tell you a different story than the ones to tell their media to tell the world simply for commendation in order to attract investors or get foreign loans. The Dunkwa community is known for the production of cocoa but it will shock you to discover how difficult is it for them in term of health facilities and the worst is the distance children have to cover on foot to go to school.

Like the Delta state always mining or the oil extracting communities are the receiving end. Most lack electricity, good drinking water, and health facilities. Pregnant women have to travel a distance on the back of donkeys or by canoes before they can attend a clinic or a midwife who lives 10km distance. Why should things be so in Africa? The answer is corruption! Corruption hampers development as well. Corruption by the state apparatus and most leadership in Africa are gaining ascendency and the culprits becoming more professional in their plundering profession in the name of bureaucracy. Why would you begrudge them when the national cakes are shared by few who take our moneys into their offshore accounts and to other places international bank?

Most of Africa political leaders and their style of governance only exist to plunder the states in order to fill their greedy coffers without a dim of the continent interest at heart. Africa is not being robbed by the Western economic policies which impoverish the continent. But what is more shocking are the Africa leadership themselves who have PhDs in corruption and bribery. Some are the wolves never satisfied with all that they've amassed in leaving Africa impoverish and under developed. greediness.

Corruption is ethical aberration and a menace to national development, prevalent social disease which destroys moral conscience and making people insensitive to the rising needs and challenges of a better Africa for all. It has become as they say in parlance 'one man no chop'. Corruption has disfigured Africa with poverty and bad governance in the name of personal interest on the altar of social or democratic governance with transparency and moral fortitude. We pray the time that Africa leaderships and institutions will be rid of corruption.

Africa is what it is today because of our ignorance of corruption and its consequences. It sears the conscience of any moral or ethical obligation which fails to know and understands that corruption is exploitation for personal interest.

I remember when growing as a boy whenever our mothers took us to the children's clinic they were provided with some vegetable oil, cereals, rice and other stuffs to help their kids have a balance diet. These items were free of charge and were written on them 'not to be sold'. Yet they found their way in various markets market in Ghana. So they question is 'who were behind these deals?' even the security agents knew that such practices goes on but who has been apprehended?

This tells you the level of the institutional corruption happening before our very eyes. Hospital drugs end up in private drug stores. Are the executives aware of all such practices? A lady-friend of mine went to apply for a job but was told by the director to meet him a certain hotel. The menace of corruption in Africa is without limit. It is sad to say that he Christian Church or various religious institutions which suppose to be the bastion of truth and honesty ain some quarters are experiencing sacrilege through the enticement of corruption. Most of our security institutions especially the police service are having a lot of the bad ones among the genuine and the exemplary ones.

Crossing our boarders either at Afloa, Kofi Badu Kurom and the rest have their story to tell. Extortion of money by some immigration officers before allowing people or goods are not news. Even in broad daylight some securities have the courtesy to extort money. It is a common practice in most of African boarders and I dare say this with authority because they are true. Corruption in Africa has become a household name and people say it without shame or second thought. Why? The answer is simply this corruption has virtually become a norm.

In some instances people have to bribe their way before getting admission to schools. There is rottenness in every part of our society. The contagious acceleration of corruption due to poverty and desperation is alarming. Corruption is a major challenge to governance and development in Africa. It undermines the capacity that the African states can deliver services efficiently.

The pervasiveness of corruption in some of the African states especially those in the sub-Saharan Africa is a worry. The 2007 Global Integrity Report affirmed that developed countries are still enmeshed in corruption. The former United Nation Secretary General Kofi Annan made a mention that 'corruption causes enormous harm by impoverishing national economies, threatening democratic institutions, undermining the rule of law and facilitating terrorism (Webb 2005).

It is so shocking to see how Africa is plundered by some political leaders and their executives. They are clever in doing this by destroying the our institutions which are supposed to do checks and balance by infiltrating them with their cohorts and bribery in order to have their way and interest pursued without apprehension.

Ghana, Nigeria, Ivory Coast, Guinea, Liberia and most African states are riddled with corruption. But Africa must not forget that corruption is one of the major reasons of political tensions, poverty and wars in Africa. Recently President Atta Mills government have been rocked with 'the Wayome scandal' which seems to take a syndicate style. But who has the political will to let justice prevail? Never forget the cautionary note 'If I fall you fall'. All the past leadership in Ghana has not come out clean from the infection of corruption—a social disease African's finds it very difficult to out-root from the system.

You ask yourself 'is it because of the level of poverty, ignorance and the indifference which has left Africa always vulnerable to corruption from the highest to the lowest, from the political echelon to the very sanctity of some priesthood, clergies and some religious institutions? The ratios of the healthy ones who are not really infected are minimal.

When was the genesis of corruption in Africa?'

Was it something we learnt from the colonial administrators in the way to scheme up things in order to have one's interest through? Or has it a psychological dimension of survival? Then, if 'survival' is the nucleus of corruption then I am really afraid that the scale of this social menace will continue to be contagious as long as poverty remains one of the highest throes of Africa.

But if it is partly so, then what about the big gurus with their millions yet never satisfied? 'The destruction of the poor is poverty but the destruction of the soul is vanity'. Yet how difficult is the ethical and moral values which lacks meaning and truth because

Greed is a natural instinct and only those who understand the meaning of contentment and happiness as not depending of what one have or have not are conquerors.

Happiness is the understanding of life. But this is what a civil worker said 'that how can you expect a civil worker whose salary is not enough to cater for his children and sends them to school?

It is undoubtedly true that all the new African states with their government's inherited huge challenges over centuries of slavery. The racial prejudice, divide and rule strategies, colonial-mentality of subservient, and a whole lot which impacted the continent negatively. In spite of these challenges we must not forget the words of Dr. Nkrumah 'that the Blackman is capable of managing his own affairs'.

In his inaugural address on the 26th March 1957, Dr. Kwame Nkrumah sounded a cautionary note '*From now on we must change our attitude and our minds . . . .*' Was he apprehensive of some attitudinal or ethical tendencies on our part as a continent which could dent the African image in the eyes of our colonial masters?

It had been suggested that when Dr. Nkrumah became President of Ghana, the country had more promising economy compared to Spain and certainly as South Korea, if not better. But poor economic management and corruption also helped to deteriorate the economy. Various military governments that came to power through Coup D'état none were not tainted. The state of Ghana is engulfed with corruption from the head to the foot.

CHAPTER TWO

REFLECTIONS

It will be purely parochial to approach Africa's dilemmas from a simplistic perspective because we have a complex problems which are multifaceted. Notwithstanding these, no pretence of credible excuses can absolve Africa from the harsh level poverty, hardships, culture of corruption and the institutional failures and political decadence which has made Africa underdeveloped. These economical, financial and social challenges offers Africa complexities the opportunity to stretch forth our imaginations cutting-edge solutions with creative ideas in order to salvage the sinking ship of Africa's abysmal performance. Africa has become a debilitative patient with multiple sclerosis that needs urgent economic remedy and institutional reforms to save the continent which once was the cradle of ancient civilization.

The level of poverty in Africa so deep and engulfing in spite of the abundance of tapped or untapped natural resources of the continent call a lot into question. In milieu of these critical conditions should jolt Africa leadership to a more serious introspective analysis, comprehensively and comparatively on the *hows* and the *whys* of the underdevelopment debacle leading to such a social plunge. I believe as people the time is long due for Africa to step outside the entrenched apathetic confinement and the culture of corruption into a state of progressive responsible frame for development and success rather than always remaining in a state of obsolete ideas.

The birth of most nationhood has struggle antecedents which led to their birth as a state. For instance after The Second World War and the civil Rights Movement in America saw a lot of changes which precipitated for Africa struggle for independence from colonial domination. During the the mid 60's to the 70's most of the African states had gained their independence and this ignited a fire of hope in the hearts of Africans comparatively in view of what the failed in many areas like the basic social needs in the area of access to health care, education, housing and adequate employment opportunities.

Therefore you can imagine the hopes and aspirations Africa posed in their new found leaders, millions of people who have not had the opportunity of even a basic education or adequate living standards for their family. Such was the prelude of Africa's hope of now being in the position of providing the best adequate living standard, education and quality social services for its people. Millions of deprived Africa citizenry were of the view that what they lacked for their generation the new leadership will lay good foundations that could be possible to build a better future for their children. The African Nationalist pioneers were people whom majority the opportunity of a better education and some travelled abroad to complete their education.

As such they were the beacons and role models whom Africa was seeking for their children to emulate their shining examples. The opportunity of education offered them power to confront the colonial government injustices. Hence they were the hailed as beacons of hope and aspirations.

6th of March was the Independence Day for Ghana. It was on this date that the Osagye Dr. Kwame Nkrumah with 'the Big Six' gave an awesome inaugural address in Accra—Osagyefo simply meaning he is a deliverer. Such was the magnitude of confidence Africa then reposed in their freedom fighters. Here are some excerpts by Dr. Kwame Nkrumah address on the 6th of March 1957, '*At long last, the battle has ended! Ghana your beloved country is free forever . . . .*' *From now on we must change our attitudes and our minds—that the New Africa is ready to fight his own battles and show that after all the black man is capable of managing his own affairs . . . We have awakened. We will not sleep any more. Today, from now on there is New Africa in the world*'. The world witnessed the birth of Ghana—the name of an ancient empire signifying the re-birth and resurrection of African dark ages.

Almost six decades of Africa independence we stand on the crossroad of a retrospective and introspective analyses ion Africa's performance and legacy of what it has been able to live to the fulfillment of its promises? Taking a cursory look at Africa performance in the area of the economy, education, health, living standards, political history we ask 'where are we now as a continent in the face of Global World? Are they of an enhanced legacy of a liability?

CHAPTER THREE

PARENTAL IRRESPONSIBLENESS IN AFRICA

A lot of African child is are the most unfortunate victim through parental irresponsible attitude. When parents whose daily income is less than a dollar yet takes pride in bringing to the world a lot of mouth they can hardly feed, cloth, shelter and grant them the opportunity of education which can guarantee them a future of transformation. Then you can imagine the trend of development in modern Africa with the population of one billion out of the world's population which stands at seven billion by present statistics.

Family explosion is a major challenge in Africa. There are a lot of conservative mindset who still consider that having a lot of children determines one social status. They are failing to wake up to the fact that the world has change and education and adequate livelihood is the most important thing we can give to our children which secures them a future in this 21st century world. My visit to Guinea, Burkina Faso, and Northern Mali revealed to me that most the girls never go to school. They marries at early age and all that they are suppose to do is to produce children and take care of them by going to the farm, bringing fire wood, and cooking. Virtually they have no life at all!

I talked to a Family Planning worker in a local hospital and what she said was that a lot of the people they who comes to the hospital with their children having people from imbalanced diet are the very people they surface the follow year to the anti natal pregnant again with emaciated figure. Who are the people making the life of the African child worse and unfortunate? The blame goes to the leadership and the irresponsible parents who never reason that one raise family in tandem to their financial or economic strength.

Lack of awareness to this truth do results in the number of the children on African street who has grown to become drug peddlers, 'mates' of various local public transports, the street children and the number of teen age pregnancies. The former First Lady nana Konadu Agyemang Rawling inaugural address on the 20th International Day of the African Child sais 'We commit a crime against humanity if we fail to bring up our children to be responsible in society', and 'that responsibilities goes beyond sending child to school to catering for their most important needs of care and attention and making sure that their moral training is not left to their peers who may themselves require parental support', she said.

The world population stands at 7 billion, Africa's is 1 billion. From this figure Ghana's population is 25 million, Nigeria the most populous state in the sub-Saharan is 100, Niger. In the entire sub-Saharan statistic is . . . Education even the basic level is a future dream, poverty has sky rocketed, child labor according the UN report is on the increase, with more children ending up on the street without because there are no home for these little ones.

Child labor in Africa is an accepted culture that African leadership and various social institutions know that they are dealing with a mission impossible as long as attitudes towards child raising are not considered from realistic economical and needs of the moments as well. If given birth is simply seen from typical African mindset as pride and fruitfulness devoid of its attached responsibilities which make given birth worth, then the circle of child labor and poverty will be on ascendency than ever considered through population explosion.

In Africa a lot of children have been robbed of their happiness, pride, future, and livelihood because they do not know what life meant. Many collectors of our local public transport are children under the age as 9-14 a primary school going age, very sad spectacle which our society has become blind and indifferent to. The question you ask is why should people who once been victims of this experience of parental responsibilities will themselves become the very people to perpetuate such crime by raising mouths beyond their ability to give a descent life?

The most unfortunate are the girl-child. Most of girl child in Africa are out of school, unable to finish or forced into early relationship which results in teenage pregnancies. These unfortunate mothers are not prepared nor in any financial or economic position to carter for the children. Walk through our market places and the 'head carriers with their children on their back toiling under the scorching sun in Ghana, Burkina Faso, Nigeria, Central Africa, Chad and other places are the indication of the progression of poverty and illiteracy. Some of them and their children has no place to sleep and sometimes they are raped as well. This is a pathetic face of Africa that our leaders and culture cannot gainsay, an indictment of shame to our reputation as a continent which fails to learn.

Adwoa is an 18 years old mother of three children. She told me that she states to take care of herself at the age of eleven and got pregnant at the age of thirteen. Looking at the mother and the children you the only feelings that comes is would these children of ever have a descent life or an education? There are more questions than answers! There are some places and culture in Africa where girls are forced into early marriage at such tender age of 14-15 years. They cannot read or write, have become 2nd or 3rd wife to increase the number of the family for labor force and as trophy of insensible chauvinist pride. The streets of Africa are filled with children without adequate life, home, education or future.

The dismaying fact is that other adults who have been under the brunt of parental irresponsibleness are even the worst culprit to perpetuate this inhumane crime of traditional stupidity nourished through ignorance and apathy. That is to inflict pains and suffering to children who are suppose to be happy and enjoy life. The results of ignorance and indifference are simply beyond comprehension. Who should be responsible to ensure that children have a better livelihood? Of course it should be the parents! But to let me confess to your dismay that in Africa many children are liable to go through the circle of poverty, hunger, deprivation, humiliation, low self esteem, psychological and emotional trauma and hardships in advance of their birth.

Such are the result of ignorance and apathy when a culture for change is not given premium. After all is there anything wrong or unholy to desire a better livelihood and strive for excellence like the rest of developed world? Family explosion is a major problem in poverty stricken Africa with all its political, economic, and institutional challenges. The worst thing is that most of African children will undergo and end up for the best will be house helps, street children, illiterates, and inability to function properly in society.

A practical example is the plight of innocent Amina. Her unusualness among the sellers caught my attention while the people and passengers were absorbed in their daily struggles for living. This is one aspect of indifference—carelessness to the need of others. She looked gaunt and haggard, perhaps caught in her own world of thoughts. Someone called her for sachet of water but her attention was somewhere else.

Her attention was on some school kids at her age being driven to school by their parents in a private car. This was what has arrested her attention—the kids of her age in their school uniform, having the opportunity of going to school—a dream so far from her. She stood there with self pity, her heart probably aching sadness and her thoughts wondering why she was selling ice water in the early hours of the day instead of going to school like the rest of school going children.

Her mission was to make profit for her madam—a typical child labor at the glaring of watch of 21st century Ghana. An unfortunate little girl caught in a world of turmoil at such a tender age crying within her soul yet without a voice powerful enough to appeal to her plight like other unfortunate victims of circumstances. Why should she instead of being in the classroom unfortunately is selling water on the street while other children sits in classroom learning to become what they dreamt to be? This is a picture of two worlds apart.

When I arranged to visit her parents to see her parents I discovered that the parents themselves are victims of illiteracy yet ignorant of the ordeal their children ordeal kept on producing without considering as dint of their economical standing in ratio to family-raising. To my amazement her mother was expecting another child beside the six they already had yet whom they cannot feed, clothe, or sends to school. What a paradox!

These children cannot go to school because their parents are poor, ignorant and irresponsible who never considered that couples or one of children must commensurate with the economic strength. How unfortunate are children raised by parents who lack such discernment or reason to do realistic calculation and a comprehensive analyses with practical objectivity. As always, it is the little ones who suffer mostly becomes victims of circumstances through parental irresponsible stance.

Move throughout the length and breadth of most of Africa rural communities and you'll witness some of the most deplorable living conditions people endure; the lack of electricity, good drinking water, public health, educations and social amenities. This is where most of deprived children are found. Children are blessing from the Lord but it goes with responsibilities of caring and protection which calls for appropriate economic and financial strength on the part of the parents. Where this is lacking people wanting to raise family must understands the necessity of family planning.

I sat in a taxi and two middle aged men were talking on family issues. One boasted of having seven children and it was obvious this man has not finish producing children who even before birth their birth are seemingly liable by ending up on the streets to the look of things. His colleague was carefully being considerate of his financial and economic background saw the need of family planning therefore has only two children he thought to that number he can give the children the best education he never had in order to ensure them a better future.

But whereas with the other person was still hooked with primitive mindset, the other reflected and saw the necessity for change of the mindset and outlook in all aspect of life social in a circumspective manner. Whiles the other only thought of having children without consideration the numbers, economic and financial strength which ensures them a better them a better future. The other saw the wisdom of change and quality but not quantity. It is so annoying to hear irresponsible people say 'just give birth and the rest leave it to the Lord as he will take care of them'. Of course we have a loving father whose love and care are beyond comprehension nevertheless he expect people as well as parents to be intelligent and act thoughtfully.

God take care of the world we are stewards in place of God given the privilege and accompanied responsibility of parenthood. The polygamous practice in Africa has been one of the greatest causes to irresponsible parentage. It is only a few who are able to cater for their family adequately; the rest are nothing to write home of. And this has been the path which has led a lot of the children to dire situations. A lot of people I've spoken to whose dreams and hopes have shattered usually cite parental irresponsibility as the major cause.

The consequences of these irresponsible cultural practices are overwhelming. Really ignorance is a virulent and a slur on human dignity. It has destructive potential. Ignorance like illiteracy can kill beautiful dreams and ambitions; it is capable of reducing or limiting knowledge, one's world view, or aspirations. Irresponsible parents fail to understand that the proneness of placing the livelihood of the children under the mercy of ordeal and illiteracy are real. yet these thoughts are the considered.

Many African women are also irresponsible in a sense that the gender factor also leads them of a galloping family without reference to their economic of financial status whether it commensurate to the number of children they desire to give birth to. Failure of these and other assessment is a sign of ignorance to perpetuate the poverty circle in Africa. Family planning is the least thing for many people to consider as the best alternative in controlling the number of children to be born yet others sees it as sinful to incur divine wrath. There is a lot of misconception and misunderstanding to it.

The campaign to create the awareness that a better family planning ensures a secured home is lacking maybe due to financial constraints on the part of most African governments or leadership in various institutions. A lot of teenagers have also been involve in premarital sex which is wrong on God's sight and are dangerous with fatal health hazards to these children. Unwanted pregnancies is also playing a major factor in the sense that these born children will have parents who are under age and are not in a position to care or support the children. They grow to end up as street children or drug peddlers in their societies.

The social menace of irresponsible parentage is a major problem in Africa. Could you imagine a second if all these victims had the opportunity of adequate livelihood and education what they could have contributed to society? They could have soared and impact would have been to society at large? Hence a denial of education in one's life through whatsoever situation or circumstances is a harrowing. The shadow of illiteracy through irresponsible parentage cast its shades on people as it leaves an indelible negative impact.

Many children lives have been so disadvantaged even right from conception through life because proper parental loving care has been lacking or denied. The associated consequences such children suffer throughout their adult age are harrowing. It places the children at disadvantage, intimidated and low self esteem. It is sad that many African children life has been destroyed through parental irresponsibility. The level of parental irresponsibility in Africa is a worry. The less privilege has a higher number of children than those who are economically sound. Maybe to most it is the only thing which gives them a sense of pride of able to give birth to children they lack the means to provide for.

How on earth can you produce mouths you can't feed? How the meals for be sufficient for five? Yet people keep on producing more babies without consideration to a number of factors. The level of mediocrity and poverty in our society has been so condense that in has virtually become an accepted normative. Sometimes when you ask these parents *'how do you intend to take care of these many children you want to bring into this world?'* The pathetic answers are simply *'God will take care of them'*, yet His words enjoin us with parental responsibilities as stewards and custodians of the children.

CHAPTER FOUR

SPIRITUAL IGNORANCE

The trajectory of spiritual ignorance is expensive and woeful, in that it insidiously affects reason, knowledge and meaning. Reason and rationality are gift from God, the human medium for understanding and the means of thinking in an organized way to achieve knowledge and understanding. It finds its importance and significance in its methods. In the logic of reason, the end towards which it is used defines the validity of the method. Therefore understanding knowledge is the criteria for evaluating the use of reason.

We should be grateful to God for the wonder of the human mind as it is so complex. Man unlike animals, we are created in the image of God to reflect his glory and attributes, therefore reason helps us to identify entities through our senses. But can human reason be trusted always as the arbiter of what is truthful and upright? Can knowledge which is supposed to light to truth and reality ion someway become the very road of darkness that leads to spiritual ignorance of God and his claims? Can reason be capable of achieving knowledge of truth without special aid which is called revelation—that is God breaking through to reach humanity through types and symbols which culminates in the Person of the Lord Jesus Christ—the fulfiller of all revelation?

If by human wisdom or knowledge in lieu for scientific or empirical facts is the only criteria to prove or define truth or reality, then are we not ascribing ultimate and absolute to humanism as the barometer for knowledge? The Christian faith is revelatory and objective in the Person of the Lord Jesus Christ but reason alone without divine aid do not arrive of faith in God. Yet on the other hand reason is the means of integrating perceptions into concepts. This enables us to gain knowledge through integrating the acquired knowledge into the rest of our knowledge, and thereby able to evaluate and manipulate these ideas and facts to arrive at clarity.

In such a dimension the uniqueness of reason is imperative and as humans we ought to thank God for making us stands out as the height of creation. But the lurking danger is when reason assumes the central seat of absolute; then that is the greatest axiom of ignorance with eternal consequence. For how can life, universe and meaning be defined truthfully without recourse to special revelatory from God who makes true knowledge and wisdom possible in the person of the Lord Jesus Christ? In a world where intellectualism, secular knowledge and human reason are the only the only barometer for meaning is a trajectory into the abyss of ignorance.

When the world spins on the orbit of human knowledge in the attempt the worldly system to evict the Creator from the universe through philosophical speculations it becomes ironic. But such is the nature of the reprobate heart of unbelief as it always seeks to push God away from their lives through relativism and humanistic arguments of logics. Every knowledge or wisdom without Christ can never find antidote to curb the ugliness of the human heart with its pollutions. If reason plays the role of deity it simply that the god of this world has blinded their eyes and seared their conscience. For it is written 'I will destroy the wisdom of the wise; the intelligence of the intelligent I will frustrate'. 1Co 1:19.

Spiritual ignorance is very expensive to pay because it is the harbinger of rebellion. The human knowledge always has itself at the center of the universe where mortals are the ultimate.

Thus the triumph of human ignorance is seen in the celebration of knowledge and wisdom at the omission of divine revelation. The wisdom of the world has been their hindrance to the wisdom of God. The acclaimed and celebrated knowledge of the secular world has been the very stumbling block to divine revelation

Understanding human vulnerabilities, frailties, and the necessity of dependence on God in the light of his divine knowledge and wisdom which is revelation is a great plunge into the abyss of spiritual ignorance. Humanity has triumphed in the domain of spiritual ignorance and the cost of such expensiveness is that 'the destruction of the soul is vanity'.

And so the expensiveness of ignorance of the world is very ironic, in that having eyes but cannot discern its vanity and blunders in because human pride and vaunt has become the God of humanism, being worship with ad0ration and acclamation of the error of its spiritual trajectory which has veered the world from the path which God has revealed. The knowledge and the wisdom of this world is the very obstacle of its ignorance and rebellion against divine revelation which is the true knowledge of God that leads to life and peace with God through the Lord Jesus Christ by faith alone.

Therefore it is no wonder that the apostle Paul wrote in 1Co 3:19 that 'for the wisdom of this world is foolishness in God's sight; as it is written: "He catches the wise their craftiness". In spite of advancements made in education, business, and finance in our post modern society where cognitive reason garnished with empirical evidence reigns supreme. This is the goddess of science and technology—the celebrated ultimate.

Indeed, humanity has triumphed really in the domain of spiritual ignorance. So the wisdom of the world is her ability to reason out based on human knowledge, with the solution of science and philosophical speculations, it is a close world.

Secular knowledge cannot admit God, but God has not left the world to its own devices for the creature cannot bar the Creator from the universe, eternal God has broken into time and space in the person of the Lord Jesus Christ. And this is the true kno3wledge that leads to life and wisdom, the wisdom and knowledge which supersedes and transcends that of human knowledge. The true knowledge of life and truth cannot be discerned, discovered or be found by the effort of science or technology, philosophical speculations or academicals and intellectualism but it is a revelation through Christ

CHAPTER FIVE

THE IRONY OF IGNORANCE

An outbreak of a disease in a farming community led to a number of death including children as they tried concoctions and incantations to ward of the onslaught. The elders of the community including the chief consulted an oracle for an answer to the outbreak wiping the community. After a day or two whi9le the outbreak was still ravaging the populace the chief priest emerged to pronounce what the gods says.

The whole community was summoned to the palace of the chief. The priest pronounced what the gods has revealed to their hearing that the outbreak of the disease was a sign that the '**the gods are angry**' therefore a sacrifice was needed to appease the gods flaring anger. Seized with fear they provided for sacrificed with the hope that the appeasement will contain the outbreak yet things got from bad to worse.

It was only by a medical team intervention of a medical team whose quick response with some medicines, safe drinking water that saved the lives of this poor community. Afterwards they were giving awareness of the importance of proper hygienic way of living like safe drinking water or food, the hygienic way keeping their waters and environment clean is rubbish and dirt as one of the effective means to prevent cholera outbreak.

The powers of the gods are matchless in the face of knowledge. You cannot laud ignorance as commendable. Knowledge through education saved them from the brink of extinction. Such is the legacy of ignorance. It was cholera yet they had no preventive knowledge prior to that or what it was. The timely medical intervention by ensuring prompt access to treatment and education broke the darkness of the hypnotic spell ignorance off from their mind. Poor or inadequate environmental practices can cause cholera outbreak. The anger of the gods was nothing more than the consequence of unsanitary habit. How pathetic and expensive is ignorance!

In this 21th century in modern Africa you will be shock to your knowledge of still some backward cultural malpractices being entertained. Smithfield in the 15th Century was a place where religious opponents considered as heretics were burnt at stake. But it is now a commercial thriving community, why? Because the perpetuation of ignorance is simply a progression of ignorance on the part of people who do not wants to change. Disgraceful practices like Female Genital Mutilation and of 'trokosy' a system where female considered to be virgin at taken to shrines to serve as bondage maid. Where in most cases the fetish priest take advantage to abuse these innocent victims because the philosophy behind the practice is that they are the married to the gods of the shrine and so this fetish priest whom most are old men take advantage of them in some part of Volta Region in Ghana, Benin and Togo.

As if this is not enough there are some places in the Northern part of Ghana where people whether young or of old age considered as witches are ostracize and sent to the 'witch camp' for the rest of their life. In this modern age we have such a rotten culture of disgraceful malpractices without seeing them as a reflection of ignorance which needs to be eradicated through education and the enforcement of the measures of laws. Ghana—a nation which boast herself as the gateway to sub-Saharan Africa yet has such a rotten backyard of dehumanizing malpractices reveals the shame of ignorant as virulent.

Ignorance has no limit to what it can cause either to an individual, society or a nation if it entertained on any grounds of excuses. it reminds me of a moving incident I once witnessed in a general hospital that you couldn't but only sympathize with the broken victim. A child in a critical condition was rushed to the emergency ward as the mother followed with wailings. But to the look of things it looked like the child was already dead. As doctors did their best to save the child's life but it was too late. What happened? The illiterate mother has ignorantly giving a wrong medicine to the child—calamine lotion which resulted to a cardiac seizure. Sympathizers tried to console her but her pains and lose was too great to bear. Sadly, her ignorance cost the life of her dear child. Being illiterate, this woman could not read or write, she took anything to mean anything and that was her ignorance. Her presumptuous knowledge proved to be a fatal weapon that killed her child.

Ignorance is expensive like illiteracy it always leaves an indelibly mark of unnecessary hardships, poverty and in a more serious note can cause death as it happened to the woman's son. It is very sad that African has become synonymous with poverty, Aids Pandemic, Malaria, Illiteracy, Ethnic tension, Wars, Corruption, Ignorance, Bad Cultural Practices, and Apathy. Lack of access to basic education, secondary and tertiary institutions has been an indictment to Africa's under achievement dilemma. These poignant realities are woeful enough to see a continent is not doing much to build human capacity to move the continent forward.

Africa should ask this introspective question—***how*** *and **why** did we arrive at this dire juncture?* A continent where millions people cannot read or write, children who are the beacon of hopes have no access even to a simple basic education, when most of our youths unable to read or write slowly wasting away on the streets. Walk on the streets of Africa, its alleys and corners, slums and hamlets, ghettos and by ways, and the faces of the crying masses depicts despair and frustration of shattered hopes of dynamic potentials that has not been harnessed as the most renewable energy for development—the building of human capital! We cannot relegate or invalidate the value of knowledge which is the opposite of ignorance.

CHAPTER SIX

THE LEGACY OF ILLITERACY

"Illiteracy is a demoralization of a personhood but education affords people an opportunity for a better future."
Stephen Osei Owusu

Indeed Africa—was once the cradle of the ancient civilization has gone through a lot of upheavals in its political history which has culminated in the continent under achievement. It is no wonders that a lot of literatures had been writing in attempt to explain the source of Africa's growth tragedy. African historians have documented a lot on the detrimental effects that the slave trade had on our institutions and societies is undeniable reality. The divide and rule strategy fostered ethnic divisiveness which undermined effective's states that could have developed properly. Though history cannot be erased but can Africa always cry over spilled milk? Are we also asking whether we've contributed plight of Africa?

Another strand of truth that needs to be seen as contributive factor is illiteracy and the dormant role of ignorance in Africa's. The impact of illiteracy and ignorance has done a more devastation to this continent but their sensitizations are rarely known in Africa. It is only a few segment of the society who understands the legacy or the devastating impact that ignorance and illiteracy can have on a person, society or a nation. You can never have a human capital—an economic driven force on the foundations of ignorance and illiteracy in that they rob societies of their best asserts.

Potentials in people can only be mined and harnessed through better education opportunities for African citizenries. Let us ask why has Africa become synonymous with poverty, corruption, Aids pandemic, Malaria, bad governance, bad political leadership, failed and corrupt institutions, and lack of access to health services, good drinking water, education, high infant mortality and child labor? When access to basic education which is one of the fundamental tenets of The Human Right cannot be afforded by many parents for their children due to poverty how do you possibly talk about higher education which produces skills and professionalism? Africa has the problem of child soldiers, ethnic and tribal wars, famine, starvation and gender disparity in education as common predicaments.

Why should it be so? Another answer beside the thousands is simply the legacy of **illiteracy** and **ignorance** always leaves a devastating impact like the path of a destruction storm. Africa for years has rendered waste its human capital, the very driven force for economic achievement because much is done as it is required in investing hugely on affordable yet on a quality education for both the basic, secondary and the tertiary level. The sub-Saharan Africa is the most culpable in this heinous crime. But the truth can never be ignored you only reap whatever you sows.

The education attainment of a country's adult population reflects the long-run trends in the participation of primary, secondary and post secondary school education. Ignorance or indifference to this fact has been a major contributory factor to our woeful performance in the global world. A better education attainment is a measure of human capital, the skills and competencies of the population. This is a reflective indicator index of the nation potential for economic growth. Educational achievement is also linked closely to health, political participation, and other indicators of social development.

Does this ring a bell to Africa people that the measure of a nation potential is largely based on its human capital? An access to affordable yet quality education even to the tertiary level would have booted Africa economy and the youth populace who out of despair and desperation has become vulnerable to all kinds of behavior and malpractices. In an environment where one is reduced to is a handicap to develop our survival instinct mentality an opportunity to develop our God given talents. Had it not been due to bad governances, failed institutions and corruption in most African leadership and investment needed for education made a priority, Africa would have marshaled up her economic potentials to drive this continent to a higher heights like the Asian tigers are performing. But one salient hope is that, it is never too late!

This brings to mind the statement of Josiah Stamp that '*It is easy to dodge our responsibilities but we cannot dodge the consequences of dodging our responsibilities*'.

Africa has a lot of her vibrant wasting away their potentials in conflicts and wars, these exuberant energies if education opportunities due to poverty had not eluded them, I wonder the power of wonderful dreams they would have bring to birth. It is sad that Africa populace has become the desperados. The illiteracy rate in Africa is very alarming! Africa as a continent has faulted a lot and is reaping the harvest of illiteracy and ignorance. What an irony, as Africa have the most robust-potential workforce to be and vast natural resource to put value but is simply wasting away with Hunger, Disease, Famine, Malaria, Aids, Ethnic and Tribal conflicts, Institutional Failures and virulent Corruption.

The sub-Saharan Africa education indicators in the past have performed abysmally as compared to other regions in the continent. The UNESCO Institute for Statistics (UIS) published in the Global Education Digest 2011 presented this report. For example, in Seychelles, 90 per cent of their adult population completed at least primary education, 67 per cent in the lower secondary education, and 44 per cent in the upper secondary education. In Burkina Faso, a sub-Saharan nation at least only had 5 per cent of their adult population completed primary education whiles only 2 per cent the secondary education. Among the 15 countries in sub-Saharan Africa for which UIS has data, only seven—Kenya, Mauritius, Namibia, Seychelles, South Africa, Tanzania, and Zimbabwe—their attainment rates for primary were or above 50 per cent.

The remaining eight countries with data—Benin, Burkina Faso, Chad, Lesotho, Malawi, Mali, Senegal, and Uganda—had less than half of the population of 25 years and older completed at least primary education. Regarding Benin 16 per cent of the population attended primary education with or without completing that level. On adult literacy, the data published by the UNESCO Institute for Statistics (UIS) in 2007 shows that the lowest adult illiteracy rates are highest in Africa and South Asia. In some countries fewer than three out of ten adults can read or write. The UIS provide national literacy data for two age groups: youths aged 15 to 24 years and older. When you look at Demographic and Health Surveys 2003-2006 it gives you a clue of the path that for years Africa has travelled.

Herein you ask, are we learning as a people? Are we changing our attitude if little is being done? Has Africa leaders lived to the expectation in fulfilling their pledge regarding the enshrined agreement to the charter of the United Nations General Assembly in 2000 on the Millennium Declaration agenda on Millennium Development goals with the help of the WB, the IMF, and OECD? Africa over years has become a debilitative patient with multiple sclerosis because most of the African leadership are not making education a priority or seeing it as priceless. We did not made education a foremost priority to harness the most needed commodity which is the human capital, the most renewable and reliable natural resource.

Our ignorance has been our woes; our failure has been our indictment in the face of the International Community. We keep crying in the name of the post slavery and the colonial negative impact but are reasons and excuses enough to resolve our problems? A positive change in attitude is what Africa need as a whole.

The spirit of Africa is being kindled in many ways. In a report by the UNESCO' Institute for Statistics under the heading *financing Education In sub-Saharan Africa*—a comprehensive data for the past decade for 45 African countries. The number of children enrolled in primary school in sub-Saharan Africa grew from 87% in 2000 to 129 million in 2008, an increase of 48%. Over the 1999-2009 decade, real public expenditure on education, adjusted for inflation, grew on average by 6.1% per year, based on data from 26 countries. The highest annual growth rates of education spending in sub-Saharan Africa, over 12% were observed in Mozambique and Burundi. When the countries of sub-Saharan combined spend 5.0% of their GDP on education, the second highest value of the eight EFA regions, after North America and Western Europe, where 5.3% of the regional GDP is spent on the education sector.

This is really a pat on our back; a clear demonstration of commitment yet enough needs to be done whiles EFA remains a great challenge for Africa to fulfill its obligatory promise. Most children in Africa are deprived of the right to education and West Africa has low enrollment rates not forgetting the gender disparities and inequalities as well. Survival rate in even to grade 5 in our region are lower than elsewhere.

Access to secondary and tertiary education is still limited to a minority. We need not forget that the prime enemy to be defeated in our struggle for economic growth and the eradication of poverty is illiteracy through literacy.

The triumph of poverty thrives on illiteracy and ignorance. Illiteracy cast slur on posterity whereas it ought not to become a heritage of Africa. With a good education background it is very difficult to enslave a person's mind. If education is the prerequisite tool for nation building especially in an era where every little job requires reading or writing then more effort and investment is needed from our governments to meet the Millennium Development Challenge. At least, even the little basic education for all could transform this continent. Illiteracy always leaves an indelible mark on a person forever. Illiteracy and poverty like malaria are the common plagues in our continent.

Africa has been wrecked by plagues of illiteracy, corruption, ignorance; bad cultural practices, and indifference. When people are denied access to education it leaves most of their potentials untapped and their entire life in the mercy of under development. Empowering the masses with knowledge enlightens the minds; impart skills as incentive for boosting morale, confidence and pride. Education affords an opportunity for a better future, a remedy against despair and desperation. Ignorance of a knowledge which is required is a pronouncement of doom. Africa for years has pressed the button of illiteracy without realizing the law of consequence. It is said in our Akan language that '*an empty sack will not stand*'

How pathetic that many of our folks cannot read or write! You find it among children, youths and adults. **The spell of ignorance is a trance which can only be broken by knowledge.** Indeed Africa's problems are complex. We are caught up in a cross fire of crises, stunted economy and a progress in doldrums. Illiteracy freezes and buries human output, kills confidence and destroys self-worth. It is an intellectual deprivation, a disservice to society and a blot on personality. It is like taking one's sight away and leaving the person mentally blind to wallow in ignorance.

Ignorance is expensive but knowledge is power! At the heart of Africa problems is can be found the traces of high illiteracy which has spawns poverty and indifference. Ignorance can be illustrated as a person who willed an inheritance but ignorantly was taken as a slave over his own inheritance due to his ignorance. Ironically, most Africa leaders only acknowledge the importance of education on paper but practically little do they do. But look take a look at this comparatively when they are seeking for power! Huge sums of money are spent on political campaigns, propaganda machineries to lie and twist voters mind, stashing monies in foreign banks. This is obvious that most of Africa leaders in their avidity for power always seek ways to minds control their people's minds and what better way is it more effective and prudent than keeping their people under the darkness of ignorance and illiteracy?

This had been the legacy of Africa politics. Little is being done to change the status quo of illiteracy in Africa because more can be done if only our political leaders are willing to lay down their arms of political expediency and the partisan interest on the altar of national interest. But how opaque is the power of ignorance spiced with greediness for wealth as the guarantee for satisfaction and fulfillment. Satisfaction and fulfillment only comes through service and sacrifice. Service to mankind is a duty required by God from everyone. Knowledge in terms of education is a mine of wealth, priceless and indispensable but illiteracy and ignorance are a legacy of curse.

Illiteracy and ignorance are the root cause of poverty and one of the most startling ironies in life is waking up to realize that one's knowledge has becomes his or her ignorance. This is why it is so important to be opening minded, readily to welcome positive change whenever occasion demands, a change not contradictory to the word of God. Living in evolving society world with its dynamics means Africa cannot no longer be the paradise of illiteracy nor the haven of ignorance any longer. In a technologically world everything revolves around education. Gone are the days when our forefathers rounded the children by the fire side to tell stories.

Bed time stories or by the fire side in Africa's case are now animated block-busters making billion of dollars. How then can Africa allow stay behind through illiteracy? Those days are over when smoke and sounding of drums were the means for communication. The era when footmen and horses were the messengers are over we live in a technological and a scientific community so inter-connected in which Africa need to move apace. We need a wake up! Our leaders' reluctance to invest hugely in the education has allowed illiteracy to breed ignorance that spawns indifference in stifling our human resource and their potentials into hostage? What makes ignorance expensive is the capacity of informed knowledge that could have resulted to personal, social, economic, financial or an innovative creativity is at lacking. When the status quo do not change because of reluctance means placing the destiny of progeny at the mercy ignorance, poverty and under achievement; this is exactly what we witness in Africa and no one can mince with words.

The chickens are coming home to roast! We've sown ignorance and are reaping the painful repercussions of our actions and attitude. This is the sheer display of cruelty and insensitivity of indifference by most Africa leaders for Africa citizenry's to wallow in illiteracy.

CHAPTER SEVEN

EDUCATION, THE GREATEST INVESTMENT

"The worst crime a person or nation can ever commit is keeping education from people even the right to basic education"
Stephen Osei Owusu

What is the value of education? In short the value of education is priceless. Education is the process of training and developing the knowledge, skill, mind and character. It is the most powerful and effective engine for development of a people and a nation, and the strongest weapon to fight poverty, child labor, uproot gender disparity in education, and the best means to create peace and stability in Africa. Education inculcate in a sense civic duty or responsibility. It is the only means to develop human capital to build a better nation and raise children for a better world.

If you give a man a fish, he will only eat once. But if you teach him to fish, he will eat forever, that is the kind of knowledge Africa needs. To say one is literate implies that one is knowledgeable, well-read, cultured, or learned. This is the essence of education, empowering people with skill for personal and national development. There are many different ways to be educated. Literacy opportunity abounds, yet ignorance and indifference continues to make sure that Africa stays that way. Achieving a higher rate of literacy is a vital effort to combat poverty and Knowledge is an important tool to combat ignorance.

Most people fail to understand that education is the soul of a society and we need to pass it on with innovations and research. The victory of Africa's battle against ignorance, poverty and indifference must start with education. Giving people education, empowering them with knowledge is the primary root to Africa emancipation. Educating the people, making basic education the right of every child and institutional reformations is a start in the right direction. It is through education and attitudinal discipline can Africa forge ahead as a continent with a common destiny. Education is a responsibility that every society owes its people and a legacy to posterity. If so why the revolution of education in this informative era continues to be the opportunity for a few among the teeming masses?

Education being the vehicle for transformation ought to be given the premium for it is the only pathway out of poverty; but illiteracy is an intellectual incapacitation and the downward spiral to poverty. Education is enlightens people minds and to a arrays of experience and opportunities that needs the input of skills to explore, tap into and harness from the point of reinventing or creativity. It opens up a new world of untapped potentials out of the fountains of individual gifts and talents. But without education one is left handicap and un-resourced. This is the juncture of Africa's quagmire.

"The worst crime a person or nation can commit is keeping education from people even the right to basic education"

It is no wonder that the framers of the Human Right in their declaration on education stated clearly without ambiguity that 'The right to education is a universal entitlement to education, a right to education that is recognized as human right. According to the International Covenant on economic, Social and Cultural Rights to education includes the right free, compulsory primary education for all, an obligation to develop secondary education, accessible to all, in particular by the progressive of the free secondary education (2), as well as an obligation to develop equitable access to higher education, ideally by the progressive introduction of the free higher education (3). The right to education also includes a responsibility to provide basic education for individuals who have not completed primary education. In addition to these access to education provisions, the right to education encompasses the obligation to rule out discrimination at all levels of the educational system, to set minimum standards and to improve of education (4). This is the framework for the International Human Rights on education.

The best thing you can offer to a person is a better education. Education is the transmission of civilization, an acquisition of knowledge which brings out the best in citizenry. It is an intellectual shaft which bores deep into the human intellect by bringing out the best in a person. This means education refines, shapes, sharpens, and moulds personalities to add value to their life and impact their society with their God given potentials which has been nurture d and trained through education. Educational opportunity has both natural and spiritual dimensions. It is a tool for progress without which a person or nation looses their human capital, worth or their contributions that could have been a driving engine for the development a nation.

Illiteracy leaves people as prey to various limitations, weakening their morale, dwarfing their imagination powers into bleakness. The reason is that ignorance poses destructiveness, a liable dimension in the wasting of human resources—the biggest liability for human redundancy. Education broadens ones horizon and outlook of life. It shapes and transforms our worldview. It helps people to make informed decisions in contingence with the information they accrued. As the sculptor by his tools shapes a piece of wood into a beautiful piece of art, and the potter also moulds clay into a wonderful form of art so does education to human the life and personality. Education and discipline is a recipe for success but illiteracy is a disservice. Education, buoyed by moral discipline and godly characters by far is the best. But education without conscience is like placing an open grenade in the hands of a fool.

Knowledge and ignorance are worlds apart from each other. One secret of the developed nations is that they always educative oriented, investing much in education and research exhausting every avenue to excel. Ignorance on its part unashamedly will not revise its way but sits on its toes with its lack and limitations so defiant and arrogant. Civilization is rooted in the craving for transformation and progress knowledge and wisdom, but ignorance sees nothing wrong with its abysmal attitude. Ignorance holds its victims potentials at ransom whereas illiteracy locks mental projection. Had illiterates had the best opportunities in education as the rest of their counterparts, maybe they could have even excelled far better than their counterparts.

Hence, the denying of a person the opportunity of education is the most heinous crime, and a nightmare which ought to be considered as an unpardonable crime to humanity. To deny one the opportunity of education means stolen one livelihood, destiny, happiness and dignity away. It should be seen as an act of cruelty. But sadly, due to ignorance and poverty the reigns of illiteracy holds its sway in Africa unabated. Can you imagine the magnitude benefits of education? Having the opportunity of being taught to become what one dreams to be? Indeed education is a blessing. It is the means of offering a person an opportunity for excellence, coached, nurtured, trained and directed towards the path of one's destination of choice, a dream land!

Intellectual development is part of our God given rights; it is an innate call of curiosity towards excellence, progress and development. In such regard, education becomes an indispensable tool of merit 'a san quoi none'. Education enlightens, it is the medium through which we acquire knowledge and skills. As knowledge is light so ignorant is an obscurity in disguise. Knowledge is the path to development, an aperture to see beyond the frontiers of nature.

Thus a desire to opens one's mind is the only way of ridding ignorance through education, and this is a virtue in itself. A closed eye even in daytime will certainly stumbles at daylight and that is the characteristics of ignorance. Ignorance is a life in vague, a limitation with no fringe of interest to expand life and mental boundaries for progress. This is the similitude of mediocrity, a complete indifference—a real characteristic of ignorance.

Knowledge is the most effective tool to eradicate poverty in Africa and education is the means to empower the people with skills since that is the only means to build resourceful human capital to develop the continent and the economy. Reluctance to make a positive change is a demonstration of ignorance and it comes with severe consequence. This brings us to the subject of education and its significance as oppose to ignorance and illiteracy. The best thing you can offer to a person is a better education. Education is the transmission of civilization, an acquisition of knowledge which brings out the best in citizenry. It is an intellectual shaft which bores deep into the human intellect by bringing out the best in a person.

Education refines, shapes, sharpens, and moulds personalities to add value to their life and impact their society with their God given potentials which has been nurture d and trained through education. Educational opportunity has both natural and spiritual dimensions. It is a tool for progress without which a person or nation looses their human capital, worth or their contributions that could have been a driving engine for the development a nation. Illiteracy leaves people as prey to various limitations, weakening their morale, dwarfing their imagination powers into bleakness. The reason is that ignorance poses destructiveness, a liable dimension in the wasting of human resources—the biggest liability for human redundancy.

Education broadens ones horizon and outlook of life. It shapes and transforms our worldview. It helps people to make informed decisions in contingence with the information they accrued. As the sculptor by his tools shapes a piece of wood into a beautiful piece of art, and the potter also moulds clay into a wonderful form of art so does education to human the life and personality. Education and discipline is a recipe for success but illiteracy is a disservice. Education, buoyed by moral discipline and godly characters by far is the best. But education without conscience is like placing an open grenade in the hands of a fool.

Knowledge and ignorance are worlds apart from each other. One secret of the developed nations is that they always educative oriented, investing much in education and research exhausting every avenue to excel. Ignorance on its part unashamedly will not revise its way but sits on its toes with its lack and limitations so defiant and arrogant. Civilization is rooted in the craving for transformation and progress knowledge and wisdom, but ignorance sees nothing wrong with its abysmal attitude. Ignorance holds its victims potentials at ransom whereas illiteracy locks mental projection. Had illiterates had the best opportunities in education as the rest of their counterparts, maybe they could have even excelled far better than their counterparts.

Hence, the denying of a person the opportunity of education is the most heinous crime, and a nightmare which ought to be considered as an unpardonable crime to humanity. To deny one the opportunity of education means stolen one livelihood, destiny, happiness and dignity away. It should be seen as an act of cruelty. But sadly, due to ignorance and poverty the reigns of illiteracy holds its sway in Africa unabated. Can you imagine the magnitude benefits of education? Having the opportunity of being taught to become what one dreams to be? Indeed education is a blessing. It is the means of offering a person an opportunity for excellence, coached, nurtured, trained and directed towards the path of one's destination of choice, a dream land!

Intellectual development is part of our God given rights; it is an innate call of curiosity towards excellence, progress and development. In such regard, education becomes an indispensable tool of merit 'a san quoi none'. Education enlightens, it is the medium through which we acquire knowledge and skills. As knowledge is light so ignorant is an obscurity in disguise. Knowledge is the path to development, an aperture to see beyond the frontiers of nature.

Thus a desire to opens one's mind is the only way of ridding ignorance through education, and this is a virtue in itself. A closed eye even in daytime will certainly stumbles at daylight and that is the characteristics of ignorance. Ignorance is a life in vague, a limitation with no fringe of interest to expand life and mental boundaries for progress. This is the similitude of mediocrity, a complete indifference—a real characteristic of ignorance. Knowledge is the most effective tool to eradicate poverty in Africa and education is the means to empower the people with higher skills. Because it is the only means to build resourceful human capital to develop the continent and the economy. Reluctance to make a positive change is a demonstration of ignorance and comes with severe consequence.

CHAPTER EIGHT

INDIFFERENCE,
THE SLEEPING GIANT

The African emergence is an awakening sign of hope for the continent in terms of making some good strides economically and politically as fulfillment to The Millennium Challenge Goals yet a lot of homework needs to be done to accelerate our developmental objectives. This is very important! Another major step Africa ought to take has to do with retrospective and introspective self-analyses or examination. This is to juxtapose with some of the growing economies in Asia like North Korea, Malaysia, Singapore, Thailand, Vietnam and Indonesia. And finding out why they are outperforming Africa's in many ways, economies that in the last half of the twentieth century were not better than Ghana.

In the diagnosing of Africa's failures one of the symptoms is that we've let on the loose over decades a friendly enemy which it has turns out to take advantage of this continent. Sometimes the tendency to look at threatening factors through bigger pictures can lead to an oversight, this shows astute nature indifference. Indifference is one major problem of Africa—a behavioral attitude, it is shall always finds cover within the cloak of ignorance. Apathy is our major waster!

This is a shocking revelation regarding Africa's underdevelopment and myriads of problems. Indifference is a negative attitude when not place in check eventually becomes a friendly enemy. Sadly, indifference has become a part of African society, a non repudiated norm, a cherished value eluding the masses of its regrettable consequences. Indifference has taken over our homes and institutions without leaving the social services untouched. Like fog, indifference has virtually permeated very fabric of our society. The absence of a maintenance culture is indicative of this social syndrome. Carelessness and indiscipline with dire results are simply symptoms of indifference. Most of African leaders are cleverness in manipulating their citizenry through their indifference. The perpetuation of corruption with impunity only thrives in the field of indifference, where the judicial institutions in many ways have been defective to maintain justice and order. All these examples are precursors to a state of despair and decadence.

In every society where change is not much an expectation nurtures an environment of skeptics; followed by frustration, apathy and disenchantment. Stance of aloofness only develops when there is no sense of hope and future. If that be the case study of most African states then arguably what is the point for a person dying for a nation that is not prepared to sacrifice for their welfare? If our tax paid ends up in some individuals pockets and in their foreign accounts with impunity why should we pay taxes at all they ask? No good social services are rendered to the African citizenry meanwhile it is the tax payer money which nourishes the big guys there consequently engenders a stance of nonchalance and withdrawnness. Knowledge is the basis for develop but passion is the driven force so when the passion for change is low nothing matters any longer, if such be the case then how can progress be achieved? Have all fallen victims to indifference? Indifference has the capacity to affect the heart and the mind, stifled emotions and blot the intellect.

This is why it is why a lot of our people have become so detached from the pace the world is running. Africa, having left the destinies of her people in the hands of colonial exploiters also unwittingly embraced their dictates. The heritage colonial legacies coupled with bad governance, corruption and institutional failure, have inured an ill conducts as a culture without choice in a world where poverty is part of every days life. This is the African Frankenstein monster we have created—a monster that devours sentiment for change. But what is the nature of this monster? Africans has seen a lot of hardships and suffering, been despised, abused and exploited. A long time exposure to economic and financial difficulties, lack of better education, health services, lack of good drinking water and conducive environment has predisposes the masses into a state of psycho-emotional immunity syndrome.

What precipitate these are a number of factors. The system and the worse living condition has turned Africa into a big prison yard, to millions of African ordinary life is just a subsistence—simply a matter to survive, a hand to mouth affair, with millions not knowing where the next bread will come from. These are the pathetic situation of Africa where most of the leadership out of greed, avarice, indifference and hungry to remain in power has resulted; the most incentive to generate volatile and vulnerably atmosphere for war and coup d'état. When people perceive their every day condition as pointless the obvious symptoms are indifference. The high sense of poverty in Africa has its reciprocal attitudinal lapses.

A large number of Africans are in a state of economic and financial stupor, they are bewildered and this has crushed their instinct for change. Indifference on the part of Africa is a serious indictment and a challenge we can only overcome by changing our attitude of numbness and disenchantment. Waking ourselves with a higher sense of responsibility and right attitude in responds to our problems and needs is an answer in a right direction for Africa. It serves us no good when we allow indifference and apathy to take our dreams into hostage. Indifference can be subtle to invade and evade it victims without their awareness. When there is barely knowledge on the danger of apathy for a continent as Africa then it is really a serious issue. You cannot under estimate the negative impact of apathy because it leads to mediocrity.

Though as humans are all indifferent about one thing or another but usually it is the negative which strikes the heart first with coldness and disenchantment, as it develop it permeate the very fabric of a society. Indifference develops at a gradual pace but we must not forget that it is very subtle and stealth in nature. It does so in a gradual process as it works its way till it inevitably assumes the stature of a norm. Indifference is not self-diagnose meaning it is imperceptible, herein is where indifference can become part of a system as a culture of detachment or apathy. The Africa indifference phenomenon did not developed overnight and here is the Frankenstein which has assumed a proportional weight on a lot of Africa's social psyche. It may sounds embarrassing yet Africa is infected with this psycho-social flu of numbness. One thing with indifference is that even or sometimes when it has becomes virulent the awareness cannot cause the victim to cringe. It is like the leprosy which affects the nerves that it no longer feels the existing condition or situation. If not so why with these impoverish economic performances, the state of poverty and lackadaisical attitudes and the corruptions Africa fails to reflect her path of doings? In most slums in Africa sometimes it looks as if this squalor living are normal. From most of the higher leadership to the ordinary person on the street seems to have been induced under the trance of indifference. Illiteracy has been a big stunt to our human resources; our youth are deprived of a better education which is the sure way to guarantee them skills needed to function properly within the society. It is only a fraction of natural resources that gets value the rest are sold for pittance. Why all these problems in Africa yet little being done? You can only understand this *as attitudinal cancer*. This has been the sad path we've been trodden—the path of unconsciousness foray.

Indifference is one of the biggest problems plaguing Africa. Attitudinal problem has created a sort of disenchantment or nonchalance attitude in our society. When indifference hijacks a nation or a continent such as Africa it takes sensitization to create awareness. Apart from Africa's prevalent disease of corruption the other is a socio-chronic disease called indifference. Indifference has been one of the most destructive factors, a subtle condition that has predisposes the masses into this psychological state of disenchantment, a condition where most of the victims are not even aware of its damaging effects on their life and the continent.

CHAPTER NINE

THE DANGER OF PRESUMPTIONS

One day after a visit to our American friend Alan Bell who is now in glory with the Lord, with two pastors friends we had to hurry to the Manchester coach station. They were on strike therefore to get a coach to London was difficult but we had an advanced ticket for that Saturday. We arrived at the station on time but the coach to London was on a different boarding lane which was not yet it had London in front of it.

One of my friend say why don't we find out if it is the London bus but the other colleague told him he presume that is not going to London because of that lane. The argued over five minutes yet the coach was still being board why we stood there waiting in vain that fateful morning. The coach let we stood there. Hours passed by then we felt the need to enquire from the authorities. To our surprise we were told us that 'the London coach just left'. We asked him 'if was the one which left' his answer was 'yes! 'But we thought it wasn't the right lane' and the man replied, 'you should never presume!'

Presumption has imperceptibly has become part of our normal behavior forgetting that sometimes it could leads to dangerous or fatal consequences. Presumption is simply a mathematic of probability, guessing or mental conjecturing but in reality a certainty. It is a win or loses, but sometimes it could be great loss can! Hence, never be presumptuous instead cultivate a life of objectivity and realistic approach to everything in with circumspection. We lost the coach to London with a big lesson in our mind but at times some lessons are learnt bitter or regrettable experience you can never forget.

Presumptions and ignorance have semblance. To every presumption there is the ratio of probability which includes the law of consequences. There was this gentleman who wanted to marry a charming young lady in her church but it comes of his trust in this lady he was a bit reserve regarding her fidelity. As he discussed his interest in the lady his pastor was a bit afraid for him yet his heart has decided without the consultation with his mind. The game of impulse!

This concern minister wanted to help the young man to consider many things before going to the altar yet he was consumed by the charms of the lady. The minister knows both because they were in his church. This lady was still attached to her former boyfriend without the knowledge of the gentleman. His close friends warned him but his presumption drove him. On the last counseling with the young the concern minister ask him a simple question that 'can you trust her completely?' He replied 'I think can try'.

The following day the minister called the lady who very soon will become the bride and also asked her a simple question that 'do you really love him as a husband with all your heart?' she sighed awhile and said 'I think I can try'. As they were heading to the altar of the wedding day this minister in his heart was afraid if their marriage could last. In less than a year the marriage started crumbling because the husband was becoming more suspicious of his wife illicit affair of what the pastor and his friends were trying to ward him off. But 'now I know but always at last' as the old adage say.

In less than a year their marriage suffered a deadly blow as they had to end their marriage through court procedures. It did not work for them because there was lack of love and trust in both parties. You cannot build a lasting house on a weak foundation. Some weeks later after the annulment of their marriage the gentleman sat in front of his pastor with his face full of tears and heart pierced with sorrow as he poured his troubled heart of a love that never was.

This was the hearty confession he made to his pastor a few months before their divorce. "Please forgive me that I failed in understanding what you meant for our good. Our marriage has been a hell, we made a big mistake for not considering many things objectively before going ahead into the marriage. I thought all that was important was love but bitter experience has taught me how ignorance could be. I presumed on many forgetting that it was simply a probability that it could have worked or it could have failed but no of this occurred to me till I learnt my lessons'.

On my wife part her love was not strong yet she was of the view that maybe with time her love for me will improve but another man then had already occupied her heart. Love has turned into hatred, revulsion and anger. Really we've regretted this marriage and see it as a big mistake which we could have avoided were we happened to be more objective and realistic. And now see the kind of ordeal we are going through? A marriage that supposed to be full of love and happiness has been sour'.

Someone might say with others sometimes it works for other. Oh yea, it could be but that is probability and probability is also an assumption. The road of ignorance and knowledge bisect at the junction of presumption. Ignorance is expensive; it cost a lot to pay its painful price, hence people ought to listen and not be heedless through presumptions, lest they pay a regrettable debt. And what makes such consequence awful is that you can't get away unscathed without much bitter lessons. Presumption is the mother of ignorance.

It is not wise to close your mind to reality or not being objective to life in the name of presumption. Nor is it prudent to close the eyes and ears to life-warning signals when they are avoidable. Your ignorance can turn the best of your day into the worst of nightmares through presumptuousness, and could cost you a lot of pain or anguish. I do not see the logic or the necessity involve in presumptions because it us vague and delusive that is why it is always risky for people to gamble with their life and happiness.

Do you know how many people are cursing their stars because they were presumptuous? Did they ever imagine what the consequence would have entailed? Really ignorance is costly and you should never underrate its magnitude. Presumption is a risky venture; it thrives on ignorance and careless assumption of probability at the expense of objective and realistic analyses. It is delusional, an aversion of comprehensive reasoning; a fantasy through mere conjectures of ignoring careful and thoughtful considerations.

We ought to make our decisions with inference to consequential laws. Evading reality and deliberate omissions is the greatest ignorance whence the law of consequence abides as precautionary reminders. Consequences as a traffic director who warn people not to be presumptuous, lest when the chicken comes home to roost, it is there and then that certain truths are realized but very late to amend. And I tell you, it would be painful to pay!

In some cases you may come out but it will be like passing through inferno till you are left psychologically and emotionally bruised. As a pastor we often come across cases of similar sorts and here are few serving as a warning to presumptions. Presumptions are dangerous and can cost you a lot. Many couples are going through some marital crisis for having being presumptuous at the early settings of their marriage. However, if they had reflected objectively and realistically they could have averted the unnecessary. These and many factors are some of the reason why we are witnessing a lot of divorce cases nowadays because people are fond of presumptions.

Life is not a game of chance in order to presume upon concrete issues. Ignorance is expensive, you cannot joke or presume about things, in that it is like unknowingly stepping on a high voltage live-wire, though ignorant yet you won't be spared by contact. Hence that old adage says 'think before you leap' is always a timely precaution heed.

The law of consequence may not be obvious yet it exists. It is exacting, unbending, unyielding, and demanding. You cannot to trivialize or temper with it because its objective essence is a wielding force that do not when tempered with it. Consequence would not absolve you whether you were ignorant or deliberate. I know someone who took his life due to his presumptuousness. Sometimes we do not envisage those little mistakes as potential. Yet people keep on being presumptuous in many ways.

What, if what you presumed to work out prove to be the contrary? The fact that you presume could also be otherwise. Should this happen have you ever given it a thoughtful consideration in your presumptions? Are you presumptuous, what are you presuming and how do you presume things? It is not wise to say 'now I know but always at last'. Yet irrationally, we become victims to our caprices and whims. Though we are imperfect and cannot always judge aright but it is always prudent to be circumspective, objective and realistic in every decision we make bearing in mind that there is a cause and there is effect over every decisions make and every action you do. Sometimes what you don't anticipate or ignorant of due to presumptions will surface to tell you that presumptions are dangerous and expensive indeed.

www.ingramcontent.com/pod-product-compliance
Lightning Source LLC
Chambersburg PA
CBHW021252280526
45784CB00005B/2335